Published by Sara McInerney Hauck

Copyright © 2023 by Facing Fear with Sara
Cover and internal design © 2023 by The Smola Studio
Written by Sara McInerney Hauck
Illustrated by Kevin Smola

All rights reserved. In accordance with the U.S. Copyright Act of 1976, the scanning, uploading and electronic sharing of any part of this book without permission of the author constitutes unlawful piracy and theft of intellectual property. If you would like to use material from the book, other than for review purposes, prior written permission must be obtained by contacting the author at facingfearwithsara.com. If you share the book on social media, please tag the creators @saramcinerneyhauck, @facingfearwithsara and @thesmolastudio.

Thank you for your support of the author's rights.

ISBN: 9798864606469
Imprint: Independently published
facingfearwithsara.com

Praise for
DOES CARCINOMA MEAN CANCER?

The illustrations capture the full range of emotions that one could expect under these circumstances. Sara does an incredible job of taking the reader through her medical journey in a unique and heartfelt manner. I highly recommend this book for anyone who is personally going through or supporting someone going through a cancer diagnosis.

Cam Ayala
Reality TV Personality & Lymphedema Advocate

It feels as if you are sitting with Sara and Jacob as they maneuver the earth shattering news of breast cancer. Her ability to bring the audience into each scene with the descriptive recollection of one of her most intimate and difficult memories is unlike I've seen. The relationship between the words and the artwork bring you along a journey that you don't wish upon anyone.

Maggie Hamilton
Author & Director of Traverse Fitness

Does Carcinoma Mean Cancer? is such a clever and creative view of Sara's breast cancer diagnosis. She captures the emotions we all experience so beautifully with art, and I love it!

Fitz Koehler
Author, Cancer Survivor, Professional Race Announcer & Speaker

Dedicated to...

My biggest fan, best friend, the woman who gave me life and then shaved my head 30 years later, my Mom.

And to my fellow breast cancer survivor, the sweetest grandmother and the woman who began our lineage of strong women, my Nana.

Special thank you to...

My Dad, siblings, extended family, husband, in-laws, coworkers, friends, Community Health Network (specifically Community North) and to the best & worst club in the world, the cancer community.

DEAR READER,

What you're about to read captures the few, yet poignant days when I waited and wondered to see if the doctor would call with life-changing news. Through memory and re-reading my journals, I attempted to capture my last pre-diagnosis days... moments cancer patients know all too well.

This work of art is dedicated to all who have experienced a life-changing diagnosis, cancer or otherwise. Here's to leaving life behind as we once knew it, turning life's lemons into champagne and fighting for our futures.

Thank you for lending a moment of your time to enter and remember this chapter with me. Stick around until the end to learn how to perform a breast self-exam and continue to put you and your health first!

Sara

This story begins two months after Sara turned 30-years-old...

HMM, I'VE NEVER NOTICED THAT... DEFINITELY A BUMP THERE.

WITH MY MOM IN TOWN FROM NEW HAMPSHIRE, I ASKED HER TO CHECK IT OUT.

"YOU SHOULD GO SEE SOMEONE."

I MADE AN APPOINTMENT WITH MY OB/GYN.

I DIDN'T TELL MY HUSBAND, JACOB, BECAUSE IT WAS NO BIG DEAL, RIGHT?

A FEW WEEKS LATER AT MY OB/GYN EXAM...

"WELL, IT COULD BE A CYST, BUT I'M SENDING YOU TO A SPECIALIST TO BE SURE."

APPOINTMENT MADE. NOW BACK TO NORMAL LIFE... OR SO I THOUGHT.

I'M FREEZING. ALONE.
IN THE SMALLEST WAITING
ROOM EVER.

I'M STILL WAITING...

MY MOM WAS BACK HOME IN NEW HAMPSHIRE, OBSESSIVELY CHECKING MY LOCATION.

FINALLY, THE DR. COMES IN AND SAYS,

"WE NEED TO PERFORM A BIOPSY"

X _____
SIGN HERE

YEAH, STARTING TO THINK SOMETHING'S DEFINITELY GOING ON...

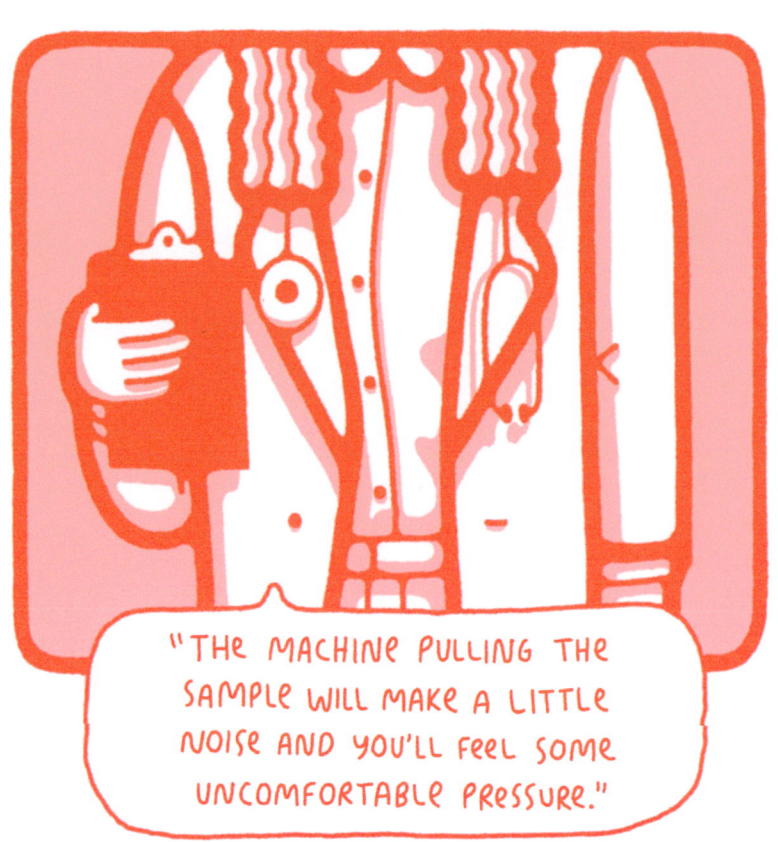

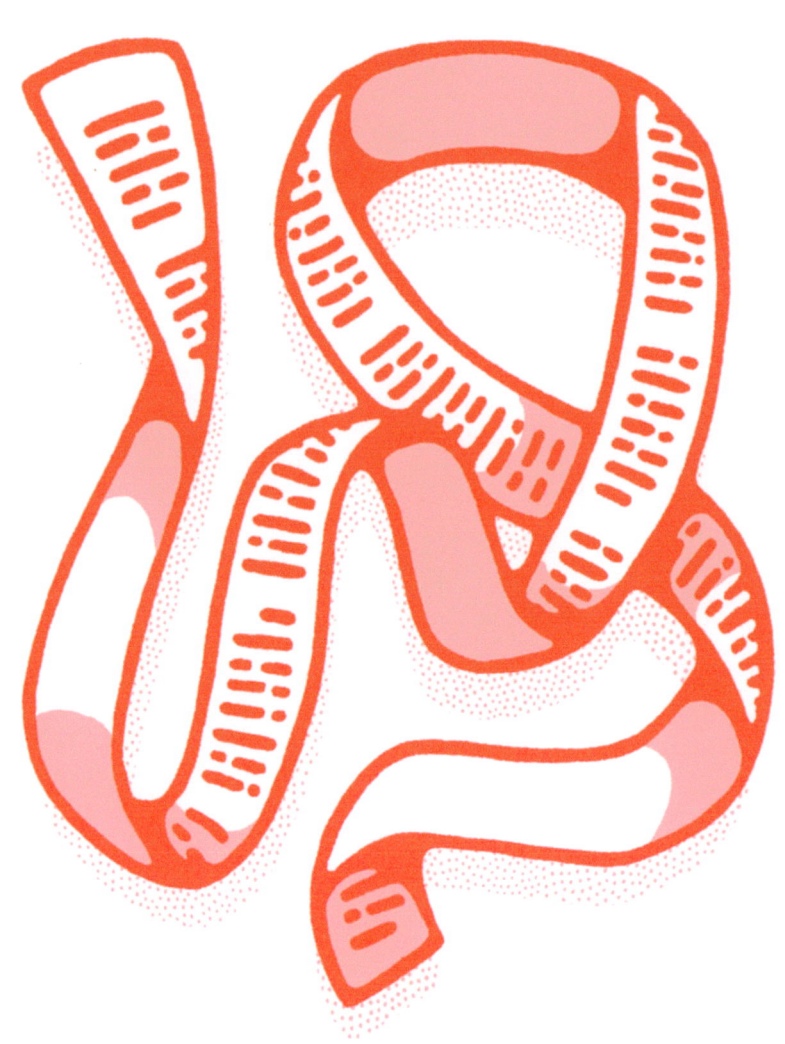

AS I GOT DRESSED AND READ THE AFTER-CARE INSTRUCTIONS, I FELT WORRIED. THIS OBVIOUSLY WAS NOT A ROUTINE APPOINTMENT.

MOM WAS PLAYING IT COOL, BUT I KNEW SHE WAS FREAKING OUT.

THE NEXT FEW DAYS WERE FILLED WITH A TORTUROUS MENTAL GAME...

THE DAY I WAS SUPPOSED TO FIND OUT, MY BRAIN FELT SCATTERED. AFTER MY MORNING WORKOUT, I PLANNED A CUTE OUTFIT TO DISTRACT MYSELF, AND REALIZED I FORGOT MY PANTS!

NO LUCK FINDING SPARE JEANS IN MY TRUNK, BUT I REMEMBERED JACOB WAS HOME ON FALL BREAK.

I TRY TO GO ABOUT MY DAY LIKE EVERYTHING IS NORMAL, BUT I CAN'T FOCUS ON ANYTHING.

GOOD MORNING HELLO SARA! HOW ARE YOU?

"OH, FINE. JUST WAITING TO HEAR IF I HAVE CANCER, THAT'S ALL!"

A MESSAGE FROM THE DOC'S OFFICE. SHOULD I CHECK? YES. NO. DEFINI-

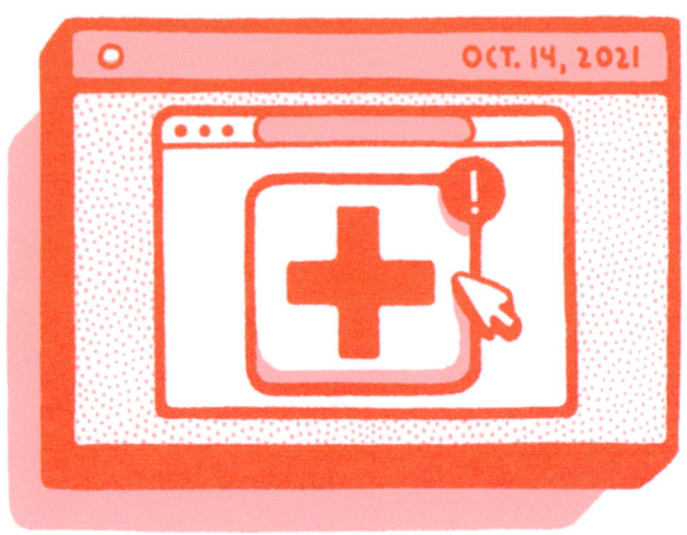

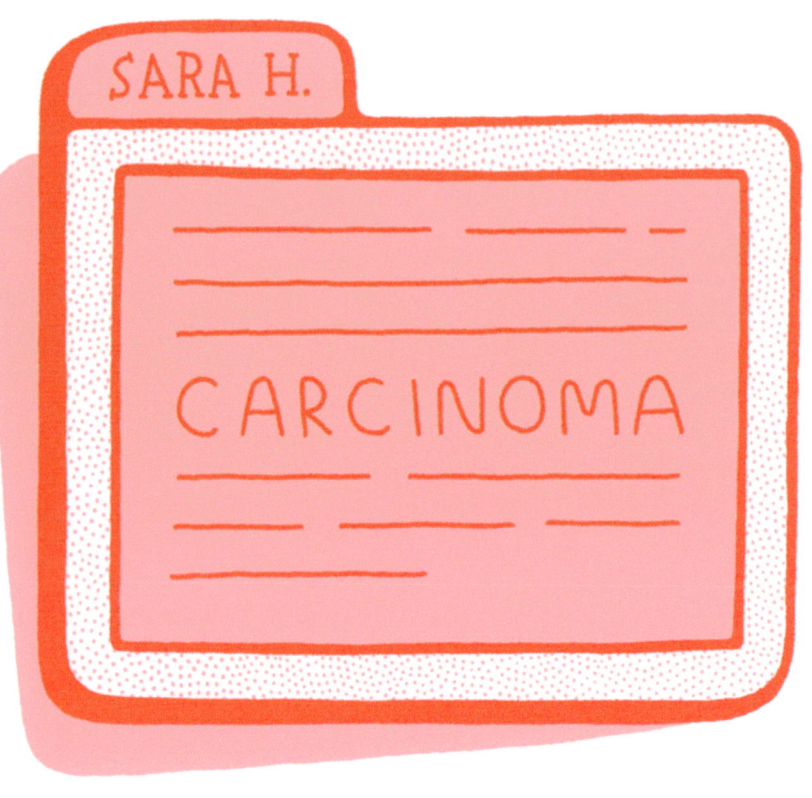

Does carcinoma mean cancer?
Should I know that?
I'm gonna check...

🔍 Does carcinoma mean ca|

AMERICAN CANCER SOCIETY

Yes, carcinoma means that you <u>for sure have</u>

CANCER

NUMB.

1:23
THE CALL YOU'VE BEEN WAITING FOR
NOPE NOT HAPPENING TO ME
LIFE WILL NEVER BE THE SAME

UH OH.
IT'S THE DOCTOR.

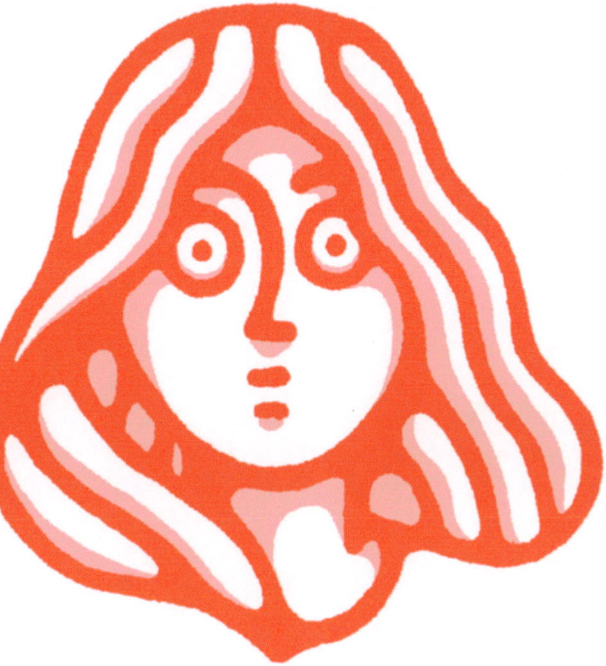

"WAIT. SO I HAVE

BREAST CANCER?

ARE YOU SURE?"

"Yes. can you come in tomorrow at 1:00?"

I CLEARED MY SCHEDULE
AND AFTER REMEMBERING
JACOB WAS ON HIS WAY,
I WENT OUTSIDE.

JACOB HAD NO IDEA JUST
HOW MUCH I NEEDED HIM BEYOND
THE JEANS IN THAT MOMENT.

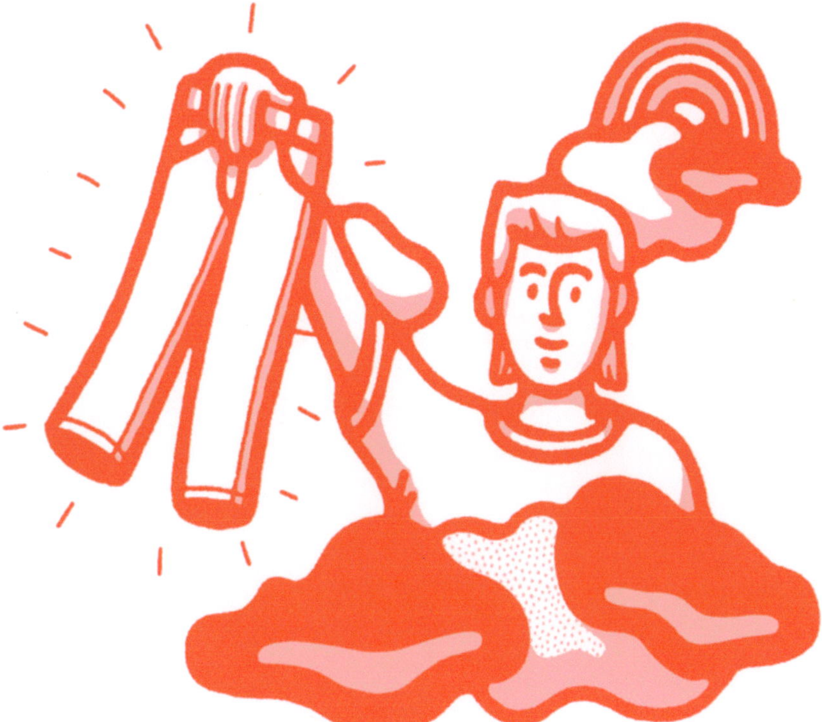

"I GOT THE CALL FROM THE DOCTOR WE'VE BEEN WAITING FOR."

"I HAVE BREAST CANCER."

ARE YOU PREPARED TO SOLVE EROS?

"SARA, WE HAVE TO PRIORITIZE THIS OVER EVERYTHING.

EVERYTHING."

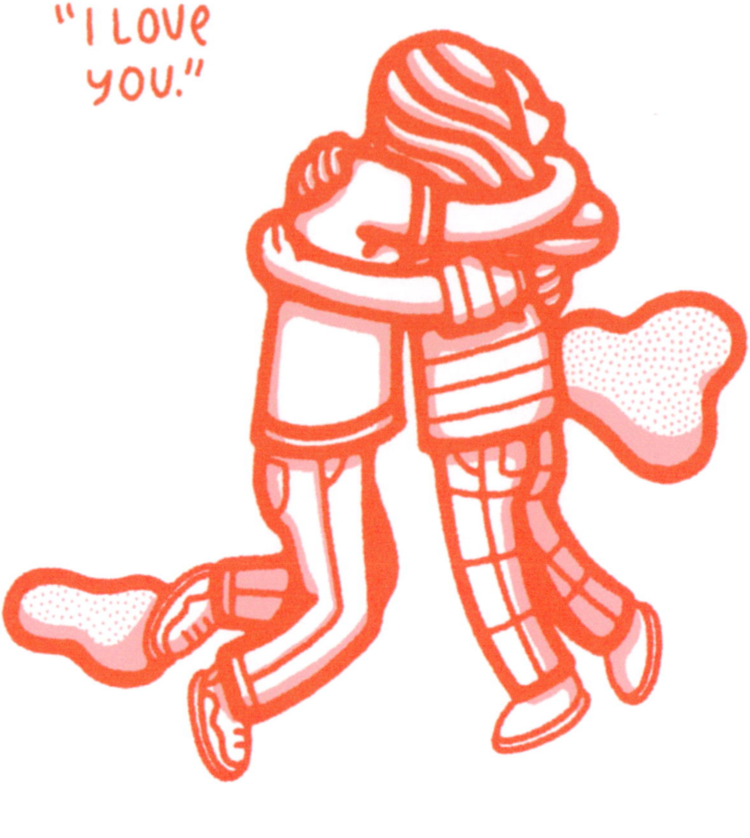
"I LOVE
YOU."

"I love you too."

"WE'RE GONNA GET THROUGH THIS

TOGETHER."

WELCOME TO CANCERLAND

RADIATION
NO EXIT RT.
CHEMO
HAIR
LOSS
SURGERY
GOODBYE NORMAL

ABOUT THE AUTHOR

Sara McInerney Hauck is an ever-evolving woman entering her 30s determined to live life unapologetically and authentically. She was diagnosed with invasive ductal carcinoma at age 30. A born storyteller, Sara documented her journey through her Facing Fear podcast, social media and writing. She is a proud daughter, sister, aunt and wife who lives in Indianapolis with her husband, Jacob, and dog, Roman. Say hello at www.facingfearwithsara.com and on Instagram @saramcinerneyhauck.

ABOUT THE ILLUSTRATOR

Graduating from the University of Southern Indiana in 2003 with a degree in graphic design and calling Indianapolis home, Kevin Smola's work draws from his childhood and absurdities of daily life. He learned to draw by studying comic books and selling his drawings to neighbors and classmates. Kevin later took up painting before finding illustration allowed him to be more expressive. His work travels between personal, hand-drawn pieces to the more refined, but all contain a hallmark of a mind at play. See more on IG @thesmolastudio.

Self-awareness

and self-examination is how I found my cancer. As an author, I felt it (pun intended) important to provide my readers with the ability to perform a breast self-exam. It's easy and can be done now since you're finished reading my book. Check out the hashtag #FeelItOnTheFirst, too!

Please note, the following information and graphics derive from sources including the American Cancer Society and the Memorial Sloan Kettering Cancer Center and are not meant as medical advice. Always consult your physician or other qualified medical providers for personalized medical advice or questions regarding a medical condition.

Tear or cut along the dotted line of the next page, post this in you bathroom or somewhere you'll view it often, and use the opposite side to track monthly self-examinations. Although the guide portrays a female, it's important males check themselves too.

BREAST SELF-EXAMINATION

The following info and graphics derive from sources including the American Cancer Society and the Memorial Sloan Kettering Cancer Center and are not meant as medical advice.

1. Choose the same day each month.

2. With your hands at your sides and then above your head, stand in front of a mirror and look at your breasts.

3. Use the tips of your fingers to feel for unusual changes in the breasts or armpit.

4. Look and feel for lumps or knots.

5. Search for signs of redness, swelling or dimpling of the skin.

6. Examine the nipples for changes in appearance, texture or discharge.

1. Perform a breast self-exam
2. Cross off the month
3. Done!

J	F	M	A
M	J	J	A
S	O	N	D

J	F	M	A
M	J	J	A
S	O	N	D

J	F	M	A
M	J	J	A
S	O	N	D

F⚡CK CANCER

This graphic memoir is just the first four days of Sara's cancer journey. Explore more at facingfearwithsara.com, the Facing Fear podcast and explore the f⚡ck cancer merchandise shop.

Made in the USA
Columbia, SC
26 January 2024